THE MIND
CONNECTION
STUDY GUIDE

THE MIND
CONNECTION
STUDY GUIDE

How the Thoughts You Choose Affect Your Mood,
Behavior, and Decisions

JOYCE MEYER

NEW YORK • BOSTON • NASHVILLE

FaithWords
Hachette Book Group
1290 Avenue of the Americas
New York, NY 10104
www.faithwords.com

Printed in the United States of America

RRD-C

First Edition: September 2015

10 9 8 7 6 5 4 3 2 1

FaithWords is a division of Hachette Book Group, Inc.
The FaithWords name and logo are trademarks of Hachette Book Group, Inc.

The Hachette Speakers Bureau provides a wide range of authors for speaking events. To find out more, go to www.hachettespeakersbureau.com or call (866) 376-6591.

The publisher is not responsible for websites (or their content) that are not owned by the publisher.

ISBN 978-1-4555-3524-8

CONTENTS

This workbook has been written to help you better apply the biblical principles and practical wisdom discussed in *The Mind Connection*. Making the
connection between your thoughts and actions is a giant step toward living
the most fulfilling life possible. When you begin to understand that what
you think influences how you feel about yourself, how you feel about others, and ultimately how you act, you will be encouraged and motivated to
manage your thought life better. Instead of self-defeating, negative thoughts,
you will want to develop the habit of thinking the best, most empowering
thoughts, filled with truths from God's Word.

While it may seem simple and natural to connect good thoughts to good
actions, it really does take some work and on-purpose decision making to
block out negative thoughts and bring them captive to the obedience of
Christ (2 Corinthians 10:3–5). Scripture is filled with reminders that we
need to guard our thoughts, minds, and hearts against evil—and negativity
is evil.

By using this workbook with the actual book, you will be a step closer
to exercising your brain muscles and helping them gain control of your
thought life.

Begin each chapter of the workbook after you've read the correspond-
ing chapter in the book. Then take time to reflect upon and answer each
question honestly and seriously.

Mind Check starts off each chapter to help you prepare your mind for
the lessons discussed in the chapters and to help you get ready for the
work ahead. The Mind Connection section applies directly to the book and

summarizes the chapter while giving you exercises to think more deeply about the main points of the chapter. The last section of the workbook, Make the Connection, is designed to help you think of concrete steps to apply the chapter's main points to your everyday life.

Just like with any program, putting the themes from *The Mind Connection* to work will take time and effort, but it is well worth every ounce of time and strength. Your happy and joy-filled life awaits you.

THE MIND
CONNECTION
STUDY GUIDE

SECTION 1

How Your Thoughts Affect
Your Outlook on Life

Before we dive into our first section of the workbook,
take a little self-assessment of your life.

I am happy with my life most of the time.
1 2 3 4 5 6 7 8 9 10 (1 is not true at all; 10 is very true)

I often think positively about my life and the choices I have made.
1 2 3 4 5 6 7 8 9 10 (1 is not true at all; 10 is very true)

I am hopeful about my future and look forward to the days to come.
1 2 3 4 5 6 7 8 9 10 (1 is not true at all; 10 is very true)

On most days, I have more positive thoughts running
through my head than negative thoughts.
1 2 3 4 5 6 7 8 9 10 (1 is not true at all; 10 is very true)

I believe my thoughts impact how I feel about my life.
1 2 3 4 5 6 7 8 9 10 (1 is not true at all; 10 is very true)

I am ready to make changes that will improve my thought
life so I can be happier and more fulfilled.
1 2 3 4 5 6 7 8 9 10 (1 is not true at all; 10 is very true)

CHAPTER 1

The Life You've Always Wanted to Live

Before you begin, please read the Introduction and chapter 1 of *The Mind Connection*.

Mind Check

Think about the opening Scripture: John 10:10. What type of life do you think Jesus was describing when He said He came so you can have an abundant life?

_____

_____

_____

Now compare your definition of an abundant life to the one in *The Mind Connection* that's based on God's Word:

> God has promised us salvation, redemption, restoration, joy, peace, His constant presence in our lives, and His power to assist us in all we do. He desires that we enjoy an intimate relationship with Him through Jesus Christ and good relationships with other people. He wants to prosper us, to make us strong in Him, and to see us enjoy our position of right standing with Him through our faith in Jesus. He sets before us life and death, blessing and cursing, and tells us to choose life! We don't even have to figure out what to do—we just

need to do what He suggests. Choose life! Choose blessing! Choose good! (from pages 6–7)

The Mind Connection

Throughout chapter 1, I talk about making a choice to be happy. While life's circumstances are not always joyous or positive, we can make a choice about how we think of them. Happiness and the ability to enjoy life don't come from the circumstances of life; they come from the attitude we choose to have about our circumstances.

How do you view your current circumstances? Are you filled with hope or dread? Anticipation or fear?

_____

_____

_____

Now, think about how your attitude about your circumstances is contributing to your happiness or taking away from it. Journal your thoughts.

_____

_____

_____

_____

Meditate on Deuteronomy 30:19: *I call heaven and earth to witness this day against you that I have set before you life and death, the blessings and the curses; therefore choose life, that you and your descendants may live.*

How can you choose life and blessings? How does your thinking impact your ability to do this?

_____

_____

_____

If you find yourself focusing on a negative circumstance that you've endured, how can you shift your thoughts to positive, hopeful thoughts? (Think about what you've learned from the circumstance, how you've endured it, or how you've overcome it.)

_____

_____

_____

One effective way to shift your negative thoughts to positive ones is to count your blessings.

> Good things are available to each of us, because God does not play favorites by doing good things for one person and not for another. No matter how bad life has been until now, it can change. Always remember that you can overcome evil with good. The darkness cannot overtake the light as long as we keep the light on. Turn the light on in your mind and fill it with positive, hope-filled, thankful, grateful thoughts. As you do this, you will experience godly energy filling your soul. It will be in your words, your attitudes, and your actions. Everything in life is connected to the mind, and it is there that you win or lose the battle for having the life you have always wanted. (from page 11)

Another way to help shift your attitude from negative to positive is to find a story or person that gives you hope. Think of someone you know who has a similar testimony or read about someone in the Bible, like Joseph, Ruth, Daniel, or Paul, who overcame a difficult challenge with a good attitude. How did they do it, and what can you learn from their example?

_____

_____

_____

Make the Connection

If we truly want to live life to the fullest and enjoy each moment of it, we will need to form a habit of thinking life-energizing thoughts instead of life-draining ones. One of the simple ways to practice this is by thinking about what you do have instead of what you don't have, and being grateful for every blessing, no matter how tiny or insignificant it may seem. (from page 9)

Take time now to list several things you are grateful for. Focus on these blessings throughout this week and see how it improves your attitude.

_____

_____

_____

If you're willing to do what it takes, you can really have a great life, because every part of your life is connected to your mind.

Scriptures to meditate on:

Ephesians 4:22–24
Romans 8:28
John 10:10

Mind, Mouth, Moods, and Attitudes

Before you begin, please familiarize yourself with chapter 2 of *The Mind Connection*.

Mind Check

Did you intentionally focus on the blessings you listed in chapter 1? If so, how has your attitude been impacted? How can you remember to focus on your blessings more often?

_____

_____

_____

_____

_____

The Mind Connection

Our moods are directly related to what we think; our attitudes are directly related to what we think. The more good and positive godly thoughts we have, the better our moods and attitudes will be. It's not always easy to look on the bright side of things, but it can be done. As you make the decision to renew your mind with God's Word each day, you can begin to think life-giving thoughts and improve your mood, attitude, and life. Do you truly believe this is possible? If you do, then ask God to help you and begin with good thoughts now. His Word is full of promises that remind us of His goodness and His plans for us.

Write what each of the following Scriptures means to you as you reflect on thinking good thoughts and how you can seek God's help to renew your mind.

You do not have, because you do not ask. (James 4:2)

_____

_____

_____

Keep on asking and it will be given you; keep on seeking and you will find; keep on knocking [reverently] and [the door] will be opened to you. For everyone who keeps on asking receives; and he who keeps on seeking finds; and to him who keeps on knocking, [the door] will be opened. (Matthew 7:7–8)

_____

_____

_____

For this reason I am telling you, whatever you ask for in prayer, believe (trust and be confident) that it is granted to you, and you will [get it]. (Mark 11:24)

_____

_____

_____

There are three parts to prayer: asking, believing while you're waiting, and receiving. Naturally, waiting can be the toughest part. It is the time when we can begin to doubt and grow weary. Remembering God's Word is the key to waiting with hope—the confident expectation of God's goodness in your life. What are some ways you can use Scripture to learn to wait with hope in God?

Right thinking and right attitudes are road maps that allow us to reach our destination. Romans 12:2 says:

Do not be conformed to this world (this age), [fashioned after and adapted to its external, superficial customs], but be transformed (changed) by the [entire] renewal of your mind [by its new ideals and its new attitude], so that you may prove [for yourselves] what is the good and acceptable and perfect will of God, even the thing which is good and acceptable and perfect [in His sight for you].

In this one Scripture we find the answer to how we can have an enjoyable life that is filled with good things. A good life is not one that is entirely trouble free, but it is one that can always be enjoyed because we trust God and have thoughts filled with hope and a good attitude. Romans 12:2 is a very important verse of Scripture for us to understand. The simplicity of its message is that God has a good, acceptable, and perfect plan for you and me, and the way we can experience that is not to think like the world thinks, but to be changed entirely by learning to renew our mind and think the way God thinks. If you want to have what God wants you to have, learn to think like God thinks.

Mind, mouth, moods, attitudes, and behavior are definitely all connected. Pay particular attention to the thoughts going through your mind, because they will energize the rest of what you do. You can jump-start your day by thinking good things on purpose as one of your first acts of the day. Thinking them and speaking them is the combination I recommend. (from pages 19–20)

Make the Connection

We may or may not be responsible for the current condition of our lives. Lots of things happen that are out of our control and may not be our fault, but one thing is for sure: We don't have to take it lying down. In other words, we can come against things that are not proper by refusing to let them overwhelm us, and by having an attitude that we will overcome all obstacles with God's help. In order for that to happen, we cannot look at our problems and think, *This will never change*, or *Poor me. Why did this have to happen to me? Now my life is ruined.* We can feel sorry for ourselves and make excuses, but as long as we do, we will not make any progress. (from page 17)

Refuse to live a pitiful, powerless life! Whatever you've been through or where you are right now, God can give you His grace to take responsibility for your life and begin taking simple steps toward improving it. To help you get started, choose at least one of the following biblical affirmations and post it to your wall, phone, desk, or all three, so you can remember to think about it and say it throughout the day. Write down other mind-renewing statements you find as you spend time studying God's Word. You'll find many amazing promises from Him for you that will change your life!

This is the day God has made, and I am going to enjoy it. (Psalm 118:24)
I can handle whatever comes my way today through Christ Who is my strength. (Philippians 4:13)
Today, I am energetic and creative. (Isaiah 40:31; John 14:26; Ephesians 3:20–21)
I have favor with God and man everywhere I go. (Psalm 30:7; Proverbs 3:4)

Everything I lay my hand to prospers and succeeds. (Genesis 39:3; Joshua 1:8; Psalm 1:3)

I enjoy being a blessing to others. (Romans 15:2; 2 Corinthians 9:7–8; 1 Thessalonians 5:10)

I am thankful for all that God has done for me. (Psalm 100:4; 103)

God is working on my problems, and I can wait patiently because His timing is perfect. (Romans 8:28; 1 Peter 5:7)

A transformed mind leads to transformed moods, attitudes, and behaviors.

Scriptures to meditate on:

Romans 5:2

Romans 12:2

Matthew 7:7–8

Mark 11:24

James 4:2

How to Think When Life Gets Difficult

Before you begin, please familiarize yourself with chapter 3 of *The Mind Connection*.

Mind Check

How has using daily affirmations from God's Word helped your attitude and mood? Continue to speak God's promises and positive things based on His Word over your life. Write some new positive statements you can add to your list based on Scriptures you're studying.

_____

_____

_____

Now, think of a difficult time you've already experienced. How would you describe your attitude during this time? Were you hopeful, prayerful, positive, negative, dismal? How did things turn out? Did your attitude help or hinder the outcome?

_____

_____

_____

_____

_____

The Mind Connection

Life will have its share of difficulties. Jesus said that in the world we would have trouble. But He also said that we should be of good cheer because He has already overcome the world. (See John 16:33.)

Meditate on this Scripture and what it means that Jesus has overcome the world.

Practically speaking, how does it help you overcome your troubles or difficulties when you consider who you are in Christ? Think of a specific issue you're facing and how you can apply this principle.

_____

_____

_____

_____

_____

> It is very important for each of us to learn how to have the victory in the midst of our problems. God's Word teaches us that we are more than conquerors in the midst of our trials and tribulations (Romans 8:37). When I am in the midst of difficulty, I often turn to Romans 8:35–39, and I remind myself that no matter how difficult life is, God loves me. I try to remember that at times, I may appear as a sheep being led to slaughter, but in the midst of these things, I am more than a conqueror. To me, this simply means that we can always be assured of victory eventually. We may go through very difficult things, but following the principles God has set out for us in His Word will bring us through safely every time. (from page 24)

In order to fight the attacks of a negative mind when we are going through a difficult time, it is important to know Scripture and repeat it continuously. Don't give up. Keep pressing and keep reminding yourself of God's promises—it's how you can get through difficult times without allowing your mind to set you on a course of doubt and discouragement. When you are tempted to give up or give in, remember the affirmations I share in this chapter: *I can do what I need to do because God is with me. This winter season in my life will be over and spring will come.*

What are some other Scriptures that can comfort you during difficult times and remind you to keep pressing on and anticipating change?

_____

_____

_____

Make the Connection

Opposition is actually a benefit to us, because it forces us to choose to either use our faith and stand firm in Christ or give up. Each time we make the right choice, it is a little more difficult for the devil to deceive us the next time. He will never stop trying, but we do get better and better at recognizing his attacks and standing against them....

God has equipped and anointed us to do hard things. He allows us to go through difficulty to bring glory to Him. He shows Himself strong through us. He told Paul that His strength is made perfect in our weakness (see 2 Corinthians 12:9). We may think we can't make it through difficulty, but those thoughts are inaccurate, according to God's Word. He has promised to never allow more to come on us than we can bear (1 Corinthians 10:13). (from page 26)

Think about a difficulty you or a loved one are currently facing. Then use the key Scriptures mentioned in the chapter to help you see the situation from God's perspective and restore your hope for a positive outcome in the end. Write a few statements based on those Scriptures to keep your focus on what God can do.

_____

_____

_____

During difficult times, avoid thinking the worst and start thinking the best.

Scriptures to meditate on:

Song of Solomon 2:11–12
Psalm 30:5
2 Corinthians 10:5
1 Corinthians 12:9
1 Corinthians 10:13

Choose Your Attitude

Before you begin, familiarize yourself with chapter 4 of *The Mind Connection*.

Mind Check

What Scriptures have helped you the most to remember to keep a good attitude during difficult times?

_____

_____

_____

Think of a time you've chosen love, like the community of Sandy Hook and Dr. Martin Luther King Jr. did, as described in this chapter of *The Mind Connection*. Or maybe there's a current circumstance you're facing that you need to deal with by responding in love. How does God's love make a difference in situations like this?

_____

_____

_____

Choosing to live with a good, godly, positive, loving attitude is something that hopefully each of us will do. We should not bounce back and forth between good and bad, godly and ungodly, positive and negative, and love and hate. As God's Word says, "Choose life" (see

Deuteronomy 30:19). Choose what will produce life for you and all of those whom you influence throughout your life. (from page 36)

The Mind Connection

Maintaining a good, positive attitude during difficult times is a choice we all have to make. The best thing we can do to succeed with this is to keep our focus on God's Word and His perspective. What are some reminders you can use to help you stay committed to having a good attitude in the worst of times? (Think of the examples shared in this chapter.)

_____

_____

_____

A good attitude can make a routine job or task more pleasant. If we have to do it anyway, why not have a good attitude? The right perspective will make a difference in how we feel and probably in how we do the task. What are some routine tasks you don't particularly enjoy? Think about how you can have a better attitude while doing these things. Note the difference in how you feel afterward.

_____

_____

_____

There are attitudes we should avoid if we want to keep a positive outlook, such as impatience, self-pity, believing things are too hard, and so on. Which ones do you struggle with, and what are some other attitudes you need to avoid to think more positive, godly, and loving thoughts?

_____

_____

_____

What are some Scriptures and faith-based statements you will use to counter these attitudes the next time they crop up?

_____

_____

_____

It is exciting to me to know that I can choose my attitude. My gender is chosen for me; I have no choice in my eye color, my height, and many other things, but my attitude is something I can choose. Good thoughts always precede a good attitude, and we cannot have one without the other. A good attitude makes life seem good even if it is difficult. People may wonder how you could possibly be happy with the troubles you have, but your secret is simply maintaining a good attitude. An attitude that says things will be made right in the end. An attitude that is hopeful when others are giving up. (from page 37)

Make the Connection

No one can succeed if they don't think they can. Maintaining an "I can" attitude is the forerunner to the completion of any project. It would be amazing if we could count up all the missed opportunities some people have in a lifetime simply because they think the work or sacrifice involved in doing a thing would be "too hard."

The list of attitudes we should avoid could go on and on. Others we might consider are a complaining attitude, a selfish attitude, a jealous attitude, a stubborn attitude, or a lazy attitude. In short, we should work with God toward keeping a godly and positive attitude at all times. Positive things add to our lives, and negative ones subtract, so let's be wise enough to make the better choice. Choose your attitude wisely, because, as it has been said, it does determine your altitude. Nobody with a bad attitude is going to go very far in life, nor will they be happy. (from pages 41–42)

The story of the elderly woman in the nursing home who knew her room would be beautiful before she saw it illustrates that we have a choice in how we think (page 42). Put her example into practice in a specific area of your life and write about it.

_____

_____

_____

_____

_____

An "I can" attitude is key to the successful completion of a project.

Scriptures to meditate on:

Colossians 3:15–17

Philippians 4:8–9

Psalm 23:1–6

Anyone Can Be Happy

Before you begin, familiarize yourself with chapter 5 of *The Mind Connection*.

Mind Check

Henri Nouwen said, "Joy does not simply happen to us. We have to choose joy and keep choosing it every day."

How can you apply this wisdom to your life today?

_____

_____

_____

Read each word listed below and identify the words that describe you. Which words describe the way you want to be, and how will you begin working toward that goal?

Hopeful
Joyful
Happy
Positive
Content
Excited
Encouraged

Renewed

Optimistic

I am sure you have heard the statement "Perception is everything," and it really is true to a large degree. How we see things affects our moods and determines whether we will be sad or joyful. If someone doesn't like me, but I believe they do, then I am affected by what I believe, not by their opinion of me.

I am not suggesting that we never face reality. Facts are facts, but the truth, which God reveals to us through studying His Word, can change facts. We can choose to follow God's advice and believe the best about our current reality, and by doing so we will remain happy while God is working all things out for our good (see Romans 8:28). (from pages 43–44)

The Mind Connection

Reread the story Kent told on pages 44–45. It seems as if he was selling his joy for a small price. Consider what is standing in your way of being joyful. What has you worried, rattled, or negative? How much does it cost? Are you really willing to sell your happiness for that amount? Journal your thoughts below.

_____

_____

One of the things I learned during my pursuit to be happy was that I could not give someone else the responsibility for my joy. First, it is not fair to them and, second, they have no capability to do so all the time. God wants us, first and foremost, to find our joy in Him, and He won't allow us to constantly get it from any other source. If we were able to do that, we would depend on those people in a way that only belongs to God. Certainly, people can do things that make us happy, but our experience proves that they also disappoint us. The next time you find that you are angry with someone because they didn't make you happy, you might want to adjust your attitude and take responsibility for your own joy.

Another thing I learned was that complication and stress were devastating to my joy, and the only way to lessen them was to work at simplifying my life. You may think this is impossible for you to do, but it really isn't. If we do the things God has truly assigned us to do, He always gives us the grace to do them peacefully and joyfully. However, if we complicate life by adding all the things that people expect us to do, the story changes. Our approach to life is very important. Try the simple approach! (from pages 46–47)

Do you look to people and circumstances to find joy in life? How can looking to God as your source of joy change your expectations of other people?

_____

_____

_____

Make the Connection

On page 47, I list ten things that could help make your approach to life more simple and enjoyable. Read the list below and circle any that apply to you. Then write down one specific thing you will do this week to begin making the desired change for each item you circled.

1. If someone hurts your feelings or disappoints you, choose to forgive them instead of getting angry.
2. If things don't work out your way, trust that God is in control and that what He does will be better than what you had planned.
3. When a problem arises, believe the best instead of the worst.
4. Don't waste your energy worrying because it doesn't do any good.
5. Don't buy more than you can comfortably pay for.
6. Be your unique self and never compare yourself with anyone else.
7. When you sin against God, repent, receive your forgiveness, and don't waste time feeling guilty.
8. When someone doesn't like you, pray for them. The real problem may be that they don't like themselves.
9. If your schedule is overcrowded, then change it!
10. If you're tired all the time, then get more rest.

Revisit the information Dr. Caroline Leaf shares about detoxing your brain. Then consider how you can apply the three key points for replacing old thoughts with God's thoughts. What Scriptures will you meditate on and what practical steps will you take to make progress toward your goal?

_____

_____

_____

Let us make a commitment to think like God thinks so we can be the people He wants us to be, and live the joy-filled life He purchased for us with the life of His Son, Jesus Christ.

Scriptures to meditate on:

Luke 10:19
2 Corinthians 5:17
2 Corinthians 5:21
2 Corinthians 10:5
John 10:10

The Power of Focus

Before you begin, familiarize yourself with chapter 6 of *The Mind Connection*.

Mind Check

Review the statements you circled in chapter 5. What approach to life did you decide to take? What one specific thing did you do to change your current actions and behaviors so you can have a better approach? How did it work? Remember to commit to renewing your mind and approach daily.

_____

_____

_____

What do you desire to focus on (at work, at home, in relationships)? List your goals.

_____

_____

_____

_____

Take a few minutes and ask yourself if you are really willing to make the changes you need to make so you can focus on your goals. Journal your thoughts.

_____

_____

_____

_____

_____

The Mind Connection

Oftentimes in life, we have to readjust our priorities. It takes time to refocus ourselves on what we are called to do or what we desire to do.

> If you are looking through a camera lens and what you see is out of focus, you take time to refocus the lens before taking the picture. We should do the same thing with our life if our priorities have gotten out of focus. See your mind as the camera lens, and adjust your thinking so you are putting your energies into what you truly know you want to do. (from pages 58–59)

What do you think is preventing you from focusing on your goals?

_____

_____

_____

What are you willing to do to reprioritize and focus on your goals? Name three specific things for each goal.

_____

_____

_____

> Focus requires understanding that you cannot have too many top priorities, or nothing becomes a top priority. When we do too many things at once, we end up doing nothing well.

If you have a goal, something you truly want to accomplish, you will need to focus your thoughts, energies, and time toward that thing. It is useless to "wish" you could do something; if you truly desire to do something, you must focus and do it! I have written over a hundred books throughout the past thirty-five years, because I feel that God wants me to leave a legacy to the body of Christ. Naturally, I have had to sacrifice other things in order to accomplish this, but I don't feel deprived. I actually feel fulfilled, because I believe I have done what I was intended to do. (from pages 56–57)

Remember that being focused means you will have to say no to many things; but compare those things to your main goals and it will become easier to say no.

What are you saying no to in order to focus? When you are tempted to give in and say yes to something that will distract you, how can you get your focus back on your goals and keep pressing forward with them?

_____

_____

_____

The only way to live without regrets is to do what you know you should do, when you know you should do it. (from page 61)

Make the Connection

Mental toughness is a valuable skill when trying to accomplish a goal. We need to train our minds to be disciplined in order to remain focused on our goal. Spend time praying for the grace, or ability, to exercise self-discipline and mental toughness. Focus on God's power and not your own. Write your prayer on the lines provided.

_____

_____

_____

Keeping our priorities in proper order is very important, and I have found that in order to do so, I have to make changes and adjustments fairly frequently. Life seems to get too full sometimes without me even knowing how it got that way. We say yes to one thing and then another, we do a friend a favor, we feel we should attend an event because we don't want anyone to be offended, and on and on it goes. We don't thoroughly think through what each thing we commit to will require of us, or how much time and energy it will take, and soon we feel pressured. We are frustrated because we are not getting the things done that we know we should be doing, and find ourselves doing many things we don't even really want to do.

When that happens, it is time to reprioritize. We make our schedules, and we are the only ones who can change them. (from page 58)

Develop a catchphrase that will help you learn to spend your time wisely. I like "the sooner the better," because I try to focus on my main goals early in the day.

_____

_____

Look at your goals and your schedule and develop a plan to make sure you spend an adequate amount of time focusing on your main goals—and reassigning the other duties or reprioritizing when they will get done. Use the lines below to think about your schedule and when you will spend time focusing on what's really important to you.

6:00 a.m.

_____

_____

7:00 a.m.

_____

_____

8:00 a.m.

_____

_____

9:00 a.m.

_____

_____

10:00 a.m.

_____

_____

11:00 a.m.

_____

_____

Noon

_____

_____

1:00 p.m.

_____

_____

2:00 p.m.

_____

_____

3:00 p.m.

_____

_____

4:00 p.m.

_____

_____

5:00 p.m.

_____

_____

6:00 p.m.

_____

_____

7:00 p.m.

_____

_____

8:00 p.m.

_____

_____

9:00 p.m.

_____

_____

You can't do everything. Choose what is important to you and put your focus on that.

Scriptures to meditate on:

Psalm 37:4

Romans 12:6–8

Philippians 1:10

Philippians 3:10–14

Hebrews 12:2

SECTION 2

How Your Thoughts Affect the World Around You

In the first section of *The Mind Connection*, we discussed how your outlook and perspective on life affect *you*. But have you also considered how your thoughts might affect the people around you?

List the people in your life who are most important to you. What do you desire for each of them and in your relationships with them? As you go through the next section of the book, keep them in mind as you explore how your thoughts affect the world around you.

_____

_____

_____

_____

_____

Would You Want to Be Friends with You?

Before you begin, familiarize yourself with chapter 7 of *The Mind Connection*.

Mind Check

Have you prioritized your schedule to ensure you have adequate time to focus on your goals? How has your new schedule worked? What do you need to change?

_____

_____

_____

Think about a specific time when you hung out with a negative person and another time when you were with a positive person. Describe how you felt after interacting with each of them.

_____

_____

_____

How would you like people to feel after being around you?

_____

_____

_____

The Mind Connection

In order to be good company, it's important to be aware and listen with not only your ears but your heart. This is how you can be aware of what others really need. Sometimes it is as simple as being heard and feeling valuable—and when we listen to others, they feel valued. Jesus, our ultimate example, took lots of time to hear and see people. He heard and saw their needs, many times before they even spoke them. He is our true example of how to love others.

Jesus also taught about reaping what we sow. In other words, whatever we give out, that's what will return to us in some form or another. So when we treat people well and truly value them, we will receive the same treatment. And when we treat each other badly, speak critically, and behave negatively, we can expect to have the same thrown back at us. People who want to have friends need to show themselves as friendly. People who want to have positive interactions need to think and speak the way that Jesus would.

Who and what you hang around is bound to stick to you and influence you. It's just like hanging around smokers; you soon begin to smell like smoke—whether you take a puff or not.

Read the following passages and describe how Jesus taught us to treat each person or group of people. How can you follow His example?

John 5:1–8

_____

_____

_____

Luke 10:27–36

_____

_____

_____

Matthew 20:29–34

_____

_____

_____

Mark 8:1–9

_____

_____

_____

Make the Connection

I frequently run into people who are lonely, but after being around them a short period of time I know why. They talk about themselves and their problems incessantly, and their general attitude toward life, work, the government, church, themselves, and other people is all negative and grumpy. They even have a semifrown on their faces and lots of facial and body language that lets the world know they are dissatisfied individuals. I admit that I don't enjoy being around them, and they don't have a positive influence on me. I don't feel better after being with them, but I do feel drained. These types of negative people are also generous with criticism. (from pages 73–74)

Are you the type of person people would want to be around or the type of person people avoid? Explain.

_____

_____

_____

What can you do (or do more of) to be a person you'd want to be friends with?

_____

_____

_____

If you want friends, be the kind of person that other people want to be around. If you realize that you are rather negative, or that you have let the disappointments of life sour your attitude, ask God to start changing you. Facing truth is the doorway to freedom! (from page 80)

Give away what you hope to receive—hope, encouragement, joy, and laughter.

Scriptures to meditate on:

2 Corinthians 2:14–15
Proverbs 16:28
John 8:31–32
Romans 2:1

Positive Self-Talk

Before you begin, familiarize yourself with chapter 8 of *The Mind Connection*.

Mind Check

What have you done to be a better friend or the type of person people want to be around? How has this impacted you and others?

_____

_____

_____

_____

Think about the opening Scripture: Proverbs 23:7. How do a person's thoughts impact what they do?

_____

_____

_____

Think carefully about the messages you play in your mind about yourself—the thoughts you have consistently about yourself. Write them down.

_____

_____

_____

Compare those messages to the messages found in God's Word about you.

Psalm 139:14

_____

_____

_____

John 3:16

_____

_____

_____

1 Peter 5:7

_____

_____

_____

Whose message are you going to believe? Determine today to think and believe the messages that line up with God's Word, and watch how your perception of yourself and others changes.

The Mind Connection

The thoughts and attitudes you have about yourself will determine how you treat others. If you have a negative, critical self-image, then you will likely treat others that way too. If you think you do not deserve mercy because you are not perfect or you keep messing up, then you will probably think others don't deserve mercy either.

Which statement from chapter 8 most describes how you think when you've made a mistake?

I am not what I should be; I am a bad person.

I am sorry I made a mistake, but I am grateful for God's mercy that is new every morning.

Spend some time meditating on God's mercies (see Lamentations 3:22–23). Write a prayer of thanksgiving for them and ask God to help you receive His mercy and show His mercy to others.

_____

_____

_____

As human beings, we will make mistakes and probably make them every day. Jesus came for those who are needy, imperfect, and weak. He came to help, to rescue, to deliver, and to save.

If we could manifest perfection, we would not need a savior. We do have weaknesses, but we do not need to hate ourselves because of them. We should give other people who are imperfect the same mercy that God gives us. Don't reject people because they don't meet an unrealistic standard that you have set for them. (from page 83)

Make the Connection

Examine your thoughts to determine if you have any of the "mercy stoppers" listed on pages 85–86 of *The Mind Connection*. Ask yourself if you meet any of the following criteria:

You were not given any mercy as a child.

You have a perfectionist temperament and usually see what is wrong instead of what is right.

You may have learned improper teaching about God's character. (Note: God is not mad at you! However, if you have a rule-oriented, religious attitude, you will think that God is expecting things from you that He isn't, and you'll end up pressured continually by fear that He is angry or displeased.)

You feel mercy is not fair. It is given to those who don't deserve it, and that is very difficult for you to grasp.

Read Scriptures that reveal what God's mercy looks like, including Luke 1:49–51; Micah 7:18–19; and Lamentations 3:22–23. Quote these Scriptures and other affirmations daily to help you gratefully receive mercy and gladly give it.

Write out a Scripture and an affirmation that will help you remember that God's mercies are available to you every day, and that you can be merciful to others.

_____

_____

_____

If you recognize any of these "mercy stoppers" in your life, you can ask God to help you overcome them so you can receive the mercy He so freely gives. When you begin to think right about the mercy of God in your life, it will change the way you see yourself. (from page 86)

God doesn't focus on your faults; why should you?

Scriptures to meditate on:

Hebrews 10:17
Ephesians 2:6
Ephesians 4:1–5

Thoughtless Actions

Before you begin, familiarize yourself with chapter 9 of *The Mind Connection*.

Mind Check

How have you changed the messages that run through your mind to be more in line with what God thinks about you? Has this helped you receive and give more mercy?

_____

_____

_____

How can doing or saying things without thinking be harmful? Describe a time recently when you did or said something mindlessly, or without thinking.

_____

_____

_____

_____

We do many things without thinking and that is, perhaps, one of the most dangerous things we can do. Thoughtless acts bring mental and emotional pain, and deterioration and destruction to relationships as well as many other areas. People say thoughtless things to others, causing pain and perhaps ruining their day. We do things without thinking, like saying things at inappropriate times, making impulsive purchases, making various commitments without seriously considering whether or not we can complete them. (from page 92)

The Mind Connection

Do you believe thoughts are a part of spiritual warfare?

Review the following Scriptures and write what you learn about the connection between spiritual warfare and our thinking.

2 Corinthians 10:3–5
John 13:2
Acts 5:3

_____

_____

_____

_____

_____

It is good for believers to be well-informed about our enemy, the devil, and to know how to recognize when he is at work and how to resist him.

Read James 4:7–10. Knowing how to resist the devil's influence on your thinking will lead to freedom and cause him to flee. What practical direction does James give to resist the devil?

_____

_____

_____

Instead of being "unthinking" people, we can train ourselves to think about what we are thinking about. If your mood begins to sink, or an attitude is ungodly, take an inventory of your current thoughts and you will very likely find the culprit. I enjoy knowing that I can do something about my problems, and I hope that you do also. It is exciting to me to realize that I don't have to sit passively by and let the devil fill my mind with poisonous and destructive thoughts, but I can learn to recognize them, and by a simple act of my will, I can think about something else that will be beneficial. (from page 97)

Take time to assess your thinking throughout the day. Notice when your mood changes, and ask yourself what you were thinking about. Be intentional about focusing on thoughts that will produce good fruit. Read Philippians 4:8 and write some notes on the kinds of things God wants you to think about that will improve your mood and perspective.

_____

_____

_____

Make the Connection

Spend time thinking over your upcoming day. Pray about your day and what you plan to do. Consider incorporating "Operation Nice" by doing little things to help someone else, such as letting them go first in line (or in traffic!). List a few things you can do to be nice today.

_____

_____

_____

_____

Do you want to be peaceful, guarded by God, and satisfied? Then you need to realize that it begins with the thoughts that you choose to think. Your mind is connected to every feeling you have and every action that you take.

If you give yourself over to worry and reasoning, your thoughts may sound like this: *How am I going to do everything I have to do? My life is impossible! This is more than I can handle.* Instead of worrying about the future, you could think things like: *God loves me, and He will take care of everything in my future. He will give me the strength and ability to do each thing I need to do as it comes up.* (from page 98)

Instead of being "unthinking," you can train yourself to think about what you are thinking about.

Scriptures to meditate on:

2 Corinthians 10:3–5
Isaiah 26:3
Proverbs 14:14

CHAPTER 10

The Power of Perspective

Before you begin, familiarize yourself with chapter 10 of *The Mind Connection.*

Mind Check

What difference has practicing "Operation Nice" made in your day and in your thinking? Think about something nice you can do for someone today.

_____

_____

_____

Now that you've been reading *The Mind Connection,* reassess your thinking and perspective on life. Where would you put yourself on a scale of 1 to 10? Ten means your thinking is perfect (always seeing the positive); 1 would mean your perspective is pretty dismal and you can find the negative side of anything.

_____

Has your thinking changed? Journal about how you've changed and what you'd like to continue to work on.

_____

_____

_____

_____

_____

The Mind Connection

If you're not familiar with Anne Frank's story, take some time to look her up. She kept a diary about her family's plight during the Holocaust and while in concentration camps. And while one might think this would be a horrific account filled with dismay, it is not. Each day—even in the midst of horrific conditions—Anne Frank had to make a choice to think positively; she chose to think right.

On most days, what do you choose to think about—positive or negative things? Why?

_____

_____

_____

Was Anne Frank just an optimistic girl who happened to be born with a great outlook on life? She may have had a few "happy genes" that not all of us have, but she still had to make choices and decisions about how she was going to think and what she was going to say. Far too many people passively wait for something good to come their way, when they should be aggressively choosing to do what is right, including learning to think right. (from page 104)

Think about the story I tell on page 104. How did the wealthy father learn a lesson about having a good perspective, even when he thought he was teaching his son a lesson?

_____

_____

_____

When we put on "God's glasses" to shape our perspective of life, we can have joy in the midst of challenging or painful circumstances. Read John 16:33 and note why and how this is possible.

_____

_____

_____

Read Mark 4:36–40. What lessons do you take away from this account?

_____

_____

_____

How can remembering that Jesus is in control of your storm help you have a positive perspective?

_____

_____

_____

The Lord sees things differently than we often do. We see problems, but He sees possibilities. We see messes, but He sees miracles. We see endings, but He sees new beginnings. We see pain and pressure, but He sees spiritual growth. (from page 106)

Make the Connection

Paraphrasing Scripture so it speaks specifically to your situation can be a powerful way of applying God's Word to your life. Try writing 2 Corinthians 4:16–17 like I have. Imagine you're Paul and write about your difficulties in a positive way, basing them on the biblical principles you find in these verses.

_____

_____

_____

_____

_____

Sin abounds these days, and when that is the case, circumstances are never good. However, talking incessantly about the problems in the world today won't get rid of them. I am not implying that we should ignore the violence and sit idly by and do nothing but sing happy tunes and smile. We need to pray, we need to be informed, and we need to take God-inspired action to see things turn around for the better. But we don't need to rehearse over and over how bad things are and behave as if God is incapable of changing things.

When circumstances are bad in any society or anyone's personal life, focusing on them and saying negative things about already negative situations doesn't increase our personal joy or anyone else's. People need hope, and we can make the choice to be committed to giving it to them. The next time someone tells you how bad things are in the world, say something like this: "Yes, things sure are bad, but I do believe that God has a plan for His people." Anyone I have said that to always responds, "Yes, you are right." They just needed to be reminded of something that had gotten pushed into the background of their mind because of the massive amounts of negative input coming at them. (from pages 105–106)

You can be quick to see all the problems and magnify them, or you can make a choice to minimize the impact of difficulty by looking for the beauty, the good in life, and the good in people.

Scriptures to meditate on:

Romans 8:28
2 Corinthians 4:8–9
Mark 4:36–40
John 16:33

What Do You Think About That Person?

Before you begin, familiarize yourself with chapter 11 of *The Mind Connection*.

Mind Check

Think about the opening Scripture, John 7:24. Have you ever judged someone based on your first impression, or at first glance? How did your judgment shape how you treated that person?

_____

_____

_____

Have you ever met anyone you immediately disliked? We all have, but how could we honestly dislike someone that we barely know, or perhaps don't know at all? It is because we have let an attitude or a mind-set affect our feelings and opinions without even examining where the thought came from or why we have it. An insecure woman could meet a very beautiful woman and feel a dislike for her simply because she feels threatened by her good looks. It is important that we get to the root of these problems because God's Word teaches us not to judge at a glance, or superficially. (from page 114)

Think of a difficult relationship you currently have with someone. How do you think your negative thoughts are impacting how you treat that person? What are some new thoughts you can have about this person that will help you treat them with more respect and kindness?

_____

_____

_____

_____

_____

The Mind Connection

Oftentimes we reject people based on our standard of "normal." When people don't do things like we'd do them, we think they must be wrong or odd. We need to remember that Jesus was considered odd. John the Baptist dressed and behaved differently from the average person of his day. Are you avoiding anyone or thinking negatively about anyone because they are different from you? What can you do today to be more accepting of them with a good attitude?

_____

_____

_____

I am not saying that people can read our minds, but I do think that somehow our thoughts, good or bad, have an impact on those around us. They certainly show on our face, in our body language, and in our behavior toward people. Be more careful of the thoughts you think about people when you are with them and when you are not. Why? Because thoughts prepare us for action. Where the mind goes, the man follows! It is impossible for me to think evil thoughts about someone when I am not with them and then be kind and friendly when I see them. I might fake it, but any astute person would realize something wasn't right even if they didn't know what it was. (from page 116)

Think about Hebrews 13:2. How might we treat others with the kindness, respect, and consideration we would use when entertaining angels? How would you treat an angel?

_____

_____

_____

Look up the following Scriptures and write how Jesus treated each person. Think about how these situations are reflected in our culture today and how we should behave toward people who are considered difficult or undesirable by others.

Luke 21:1–4
John 4:7–15
Matthew 8:5–11
Luke 8:43–48

_____

_____

_____

_____

_____

Make the Connection

What we think about others greatly impacts how we relate to them. Our thoughts about a person affect how we treat them, and how we allow that person to treat us. A person may want to do something kind for us, but if we have already decided that we don't trust them, we may shut a door of opportunity that God is trying to open. (from page 121)

Spend some time asking God for forgiveness for the way you've treated or thought about people you don't really know or judged too quickly. Ask for God to help you walk in love and reach out to those who are different from you. Write a list of people you will be intentionally more open to this week.

_____

_____

_____

Every person has a story. If you get to know them, you might begin to think of them in a different light.

Scriptures to meditate on:

1 Samuel 16:7
John 13:34
Hebrews 13:2

Anybody Can Change

Before you begin, familiarize yourself with chapter 12 of *The Mind Connection*.

Mind Check

Think of something you said would never change, but has—a person, one of your habits, a situation. Describe what happened and how.

_____

_____

_____

Think about the opening Scripture. Do you believe that all things are possible with God? Explain.

_____

_____

_____

The best way to kill a relationship is to look at the other person and think, *You will never change.* Thankfully, God always believes we can change, and therefore, He continues to work with us. We would be more patient and long-suffering with the flaws of people if we purposely thought, *God is patient with me and I will be patient with you.*

We can always choose to pray for people instead of giving up on them. (from page 125)

The Mind Connection

Nobody is beyond change! It may take a long time for them to do so, but it can happen. (from page 127)

Do you honestly believe this statement? Explain?

_____

_____

_____

What habit do you desire to change? Do you believe that God can help you change it?

_____

_____

_____

What person do you want to change? Do you believe that God can help that person change? Are you praying for them?

_____

_____

_____

Even if you see no change at all yet, you can continue believing that God is working and guide your conversations with others in that direction. Fill your mind with thoughts like *I believe God is working and all things are possible with Him.* You will feel better, and your attitude toward the person in question will be much better. (from pages 127–128)

Write your own affirmation of faith that God is working on behalf of the person who is on your heart.

_____

_____

_____

Make the Connection

How can each of the following Scriptures help you deal with the person you are praying for?

Philippians 4:13

_____

_____

_____

Galatians 6:2

_____

_____

_____

Galatians 6:9

_____

_____

_____

Even when an individual comes to the point that they want to change, they cannot do it alone. Only God can work from the inside out, and that is what we need. For any change in behavior to last, it must come from the heart. I can muster enough discipline to change some of my behavior, but only God can change my heart.

As I said, anyone can change, but God has to be invited to do the changing. Our job is to want to change, and God's job is to do the work while we believe and cooperate with His instructions. (from page 132)

Supernatural change always comes from the inside out.

Scriptures to meditate on:

1 Corinthians 13:4
John 16:8
Philippians 4:13

CHAPTER 13

Why Aren't You Like Me?

Before you begin, familiarize yourself with chapter 13 of *The Mind Connection*.

Mind Check

How has your attitude toward difficult people been impacted by thinking and speaking positive things from God's Word about them?

_____

_____

_____

God is creative and He loves variety! How do we see this in the people He has created, and why is it important for people to be different and unique?

_____

_____

_____

_____

When it comes to having good relationships, it is vital that we learn to accept the differences in all people. God creates us all differently on purpose. Those who are different from you are not just people who got in all the wrong lines when God was passing out personality traits. (from page 136)

Read Psalm 139:13–16. What do these verses tell you about your value to God?

_____

_____

_____

Remember God knit together each of us in a unique way.

> We are not mistakes just because we are not like someone else. (from page 136)

The Mind Connection

Thinking everyone should be like us is one of our biggest problems in relationships, and it causes a lot of wrong thinking and wrong attitudes that are damaging to healthy and satisfying marriages, friendships, and work relationships.

It still amazes me how much trouble I had getting along with people until I learned the important lesson that I am not the perfect standard for how people should be. (from page 137)

How would the world be if everyone was the same—if they thought the same way, looked the same, etc.?

_____

_____

_____

Are there people you avoid or ignore because they are not like you? Take some time to really think about this and be honest. Make an effort today to reach out to them and pray for God to help you see them through His eyes. Write a prayer asking God to help you have an open mind and heart about how you can appreciate and interact with them.

_____

_____

_____

_____

I don't feel the need to apologize for how I see things and what I like or don't like. Of course, in order to have that freedom, I need to give freedom to others, and I have learned to do so. I am still growing, of course, but at least I understand the importance of the principle and how it affects relationships. (from page 138)

Make the Connection

Review your upcoming week. Think of the people you will meet with. How can you make each one feel significant? How can you improve your interactions by purposefully thinking positively about them, even before you meet? Write their names and your prayer below.

_____

_____

_____

_____

Taking this positive viewpoint about people doesn't mean that they have nothing in their personalities that needs to be changed or polished, but it does mean that we agree not to see ourselves as being more important and valuable than others. It also means that we agree that God is wise, and since He seems to love variety, then we need to embrace it also. (from page 141)

Making people feel significant begins with how we think about them.

Scriptures to meditate on:

Psalm 19:14
Romans 12:3–5
Philippians 4:8

SECTION 3

How Your Thoughts Affect Your Physical and Emotional Health

In *The Mind Connection*, we've looked at how our thoughts impact our outlook on life as well as our interactions with others. In the third section, we'll look at how our thoughts impact our health—physically and emotionally.

Take a few minutes to think about how your thoughts have impacted your emotional and physical health. Journal about it.

_____

_____

_____

_____

_____

_____

_____

Your Thoughts and Stress

Before you begin, familiarize yourself with chapter 14 of *The Mind Connection*.

Mind Check

Think about the opening Scripture, Proverbs 3:5. How can depending on and trusting in God for everything help your emotional health?

_____

_____

_____

Some years ago I had to face the fact that although I said, "I trust God," my mind proved that I really didn't. I wanted to trust Him, but the truth was that I worried and felt fearful and anxious in many situations. Being truthful with myself helped me to begin dealing with the negative mental habits that were hindering my faith. I can't say that I am totally worry free at this point in my life, but I have come a long way toward the goal, and the less I worry, the less stress I have! There is no doubt that our thoughts and our stress levels are closely connected. (from page 149)

What do you need to rely on God for specifically this week? Write a prayer acknowledging God and seeking to depend on Him with all of your mind and heart in that particular situation or area of your life.

_____

_____

_____

_____

The Mind Connection

When we worry, we are searching for answers to our problems, hoping we will find a way to control situations in our life, but the truth is that we were never in control anyway, because God is. Instead of using our power to attempt to control situations and people, we should use it to control ourselves. Instead of worrying about things we cannot control, we should control our worry! (from page 150)

Would you say that you control your worry, or does it control you? Are there some things that are easier to entrust to God than others? Consider the areas of your life that you struggle to trust God to handle. Why do you feel that way, and how can you turn them over to Him?

_____

_____

_____

_____

How does remembering when God helped you overcome difficult times help you to stop worrying about current situations? What can you use as reminders of those times and God's provision?

_____

_____

_____

_____

_____

Make the Connection

Review the list of things I discovered that helped me relieve my stress. Circle the things you could incorporate in your life and add other ideas to the list if you have them.

Make a plan to incorporate at least one of the things from the list this week and write how you will walk it out.

- Change my schedule and leave enough room in it so I don't end up rushing from one event to the next with no breaks in between.
- Take time to do things I enjoy instead of being excessive about work, because no matter how long I work, there will always be another project that needs to be done.
- Have a plan, but don't get upset if my plan is interrupted for valid reasons.
- Make better choices about what I eat, because it is true that the kind of fuel I put in my body will determine how well it functions for me.
- Have a regular bedtime and get good sleep.
- Don't try to keep all the people happy all the time at the cost of living with unhealthy stress.
- Say no when I need to.

_____

_____

_____

_____

The main thing we must comprehend is that worry is a complete waste of time and energy. It creates stress in our bodies, and long-term stress has unbelievably destructive side effects.

When we feel emotionally upset, we can calm ourselves down by choosing to think on something other than our problems. Invite a friend who is a positive person to lunch, listen to some happy and comforting music, or go do something for someone else in need. I have found that reading material on the effects of stress may also be helpful. When we remind ourselves of the long-term results of our actions, it may help us be wise enough to make a change in how we approach life before serious damage is done. (from pages 152–153)

To avoid stress and worry, choose to think positive thoughts on purpose.

Scriptures to meditate on:

Isaiah 26:3
Matthew 11:28–30
1 Corinthians 2:16
Philippians 4:6–7

The Mind-Body Connection

Before you begin, familiarize yourself with chapter 15 of *The Mind Connection*.

Mind Check

What have you done this past week that has helped you stop worrying or reduce stress? What are you planning to continue to do to live a healthy, worry-free lifestyle?

_____

_____

_____

_____

_____

Have you ever noticed that your physical pain decreases when your mood increases, such as when you are looking forward to something like lunch with a friend? Describe the connection that produces this result.

_____

_____

_____

Our bodies are like automobiles that God provides for us to drive around earth in. If we want them to perform to their maximum ability and be around for a long time, then we need to choose to think in ways that will help them. All of our thoughts, good or bad, have an effect on our physical being. The mind and body are definitely connected. (from page 161)

The Mind Connection

Reflect on Dr. Leaf's words:

> Science and Scripture both show that we are wired for love and optimism and so when we react by thinking negatively and making negative choices, the quality of our thinking suffers, which means the quality of our brain architecture suffers. It is comforting—and challenging—to know that negative thinking is not the norm....
> Toxic thinking wears down the brain. (from page 163)

Take note of where your body hurts when you have negative thoughts. Keep track of the correlation between your mind and body this week.

_____

_____

_____

> Pay attention to how memories affect you. If I let my mind drift back to specific instances when my father was abusing me or beating my mother, or yelling in anger, or the fear I experienced constantly throughout my childhood, my body responds with tightness and I clench my teeth. I don't allow myself to do that very often, but there are occasions when I find my mind has gone to a wrong memory, and I have to retrieve it quickly before it traps me in a painful place that is unhealthy. Good memories have the opposite effect. They produce peace and relaxation, both of which cooperate with the healing properties God has placed in our bodies.

If I allow my thoughts today to be on what went wrong yesterday or mistakes I may have made, it will only zap my strength for today. (From pages 166–167)

Review the following Scriptures and write down how good memories affected each person (or group of people):

Deuteronomy 24:18

_____

_____

_____

Esther 9:27–29

_____

_____

_____

Psalm 42:4–5

_____

_____

_____

Make the Connection

Think over your life and some of the happiest memories you have; think about the big events and the small encounters that still make you happy when you reflect on them. List them below and find pictures, souvenirs, and the like to keep handy so they can remind you to think about those great memories. Write a prayer of thanks for all God has done for you.

_____

_____

_____

_____

_____

_____

_____

As Dr. Leaf wrote:

> We are constantly reacting to circumstances and events, and as this cycle goes on, our brains become shaped by the process in either a positive, good-quality-of-life direction or a negative, toxic, poor-quality-of-life direction. So it is the quality of our thinking and choices (consciousness) and our reactions that determine our "brain architecture"—the shape or design of the brain and *resultant* quality of the health of our minds and bodies. (from pages 162–163)

Thankful people are happy people, and happy people are healthier people.

Scriptures to meditate on:

Genesis 1:26
Philippians 3:12–14
Ephesians 4:26
Psalm 63:5–7

The Mind-Performance Connection

Before you begin, familiarize yourself with chapter 16 of *The Mind Connection*.

Mind Check

Review your list of happy memories from the last chapter. How often have you been thinking about them this week? Do you see a difference in your mood?

_____

_____

_____

Think about the opening quote by William Shakespeare: "All things are ready, if our minds be so." How has this proven true in your life?

_____

_____

_____

Learning about the mind-body connection won't necessarily cure all of our illnesses and turn us into superheroes, but we can improve our lives in many ways by learning how to think properly. Not only does the mind affect our bodies, but it also affects our performance in all areas of life. If you are going for a job interview, I am sure that you want to perform well and appear to be confident and capable.

No company wants to hire anyone who has no confidence that they can do the job they are applying for. The thoughts you think prior to the interview will determine, at least in large part, how you perform during the interview.

If a person fears failure and they go to the interview doubting they will get the job and entertaining all sorts of thoughts that minimize their ability, they surely will not get the job. (from page 170)

The Mind Connection

Take time to assess how you've been thinking more like God and His Word since beginning this book. What changes have you seen in your mood? Health? Life?

_____

_____

_____

Read the following quotes from page 172 in *The Mind Connection* and write your thoughts about them and how they apply to your thinking.

You have to expect things of yourself before you can do them. (Michael Jordan)

_____

_____

_____

I have learned that your mind can amaze your body if you just keep telling yourself, I can do it . . . I can do it . . . I can do it. (Jon Erickson)

_____

_____

_____

Never let the fear of striking out get in your way. (Babe Ruth)

_____

_____

_____

Sometimes the biggest problem is in your head. You've got to believe you can play a shot instead of wondering where your next bad shot is coming from. (Jack Nicklaus)

_____

_____

_____

The most important part of a player's body is above his shoulders. (Ty Cobb)

_____

_____

_____

Choose a Scripture that reminds you that God gives you the ability to do what you need to do, such as Ephesians 2:10 or Philippians 4:13. Memorize and meditate on it each day this week.

We certainly cannot control all of our performance and reactions to things by thinking in certain ways. God is ultimately in control, and we succeed by leaning on and trusting in Him, and not merely through positive thinking. However, there is nothing in any kind of negative thinking that would help us in any way. Even if I were a ballplayer (which I am not), and I thought I would hit a home run but ended up striking out, at least I wouldn't have drained my energy for the next opportunity through defeatist, energy-draining mental habits. (from page 173)

Make the Connection

Instead of dreading any task that is before you, why not think like this: *This is something I need to do, and I can do, and I am going to do it with a good attitude. I refuse to dread daily tasks, and I am not going to allow wrong thinking to rob me of my ability to perform strong and well.* (from page 177)

List the things you need to do today and this week. If there's anything you're dreading, write a positive way of thinking about it. Make a note of how your attitude and performance changed when you changed your mind about doing your task.

_____

_____

_____

_____

_____

Think "I can" thoughts, not "I can't" thoughts. Think "I love" thoughts, not "I hate" thoughts. Think "I look forward to" thoughts, not "I resent" thoughts.

Scriptures to meditate on:

Philippians 4:13
Ephesians 2:10
Psalm 118:24
Proverbs 23:7

Where Did All My Energy Go?

Before you begin, familiarize yourself with chapter 17 of *The Mind Connection*.

Mind Check

Review the list of things you committed to do with a positive attitude from chapter 16. How did thinking positively help your performance?

_____

_____

_____

Think about this statement from page 180:

> The only people who succeed in life are those who can do what they know is important with or without emotional excitement to motivate them!

Does this describe you? Why or why not?

_____

_____

_____

When your get-up-and-go has got up and gone, you need to get up and get it back. We won't become so tired of doing what we do in life if we are more careful concerning how we think about our lives. The more appreciative I am for the life I have, the more I enjoy living it. (from page 180)

The Mind Connection

What is in our hearts does come out of our mouths and shows up in our attitudes and behaviors. (from page 181)

Review your life and your daily activities. How is your energy level? Which activities or responsibilities have you grown weary of? Do you have an ungrateful attitude toward them?

_____

_____

_____

_____

_____

How can you change the way you look at these activities, renew your mind, and strengthen the capabilities God has given you?

_____

_____

_____

If you are contemplating a change, remember to give it the time test to be sure you are not just acting upon emotions.

I urge you to be careful about the kind of thoughts you allow to roll around in your mind when you find yourself getting a little tired of doing what you do. Stay positive and if you should come to the point, after a reasonable amount of time has passed, that you are confident that you need to make a change, then do so. But don't blame other people and leave with a bitter, resentful attitude.

There are times in life when God lets us know a change is ahead for us by removing the desire we once had to do what we are doing. It is very wise to give these feelings the "time test" to be sure they are not mere emotions that would lead to regret if acted upon. If they pass the test and remain for a long time, it may be safe to assume that you need to prayerfully consider a change. (from page 181)

Make the Connection

Check your heart to make sure you do not have strife, fear, or guilt, which can rob you of the energy and zest you need for life. If you do, write a prayer for help in releasing those thoughts and feelings and move forward. Listen for things you should do to let these thoughts and attitudes go.

_____

_____

_____

_____

Perhaps your energy is zapped because of one or more of these habits: lack of sleep, stress, poor food choices, or health problems. If so, how can you begin to address these issues and commit to getting the energy you need to be creative and focused? Write your plan below.

_____

_____

_____

_____

We all love having emotion to motivate us, but emotions are linked to our thoughts and tend to be abundant at some times and yet totally missing at other times. When emotion is gone and energy seems low, the best thing to do is check your thinking and make adjustments where needed, and then stir yourself up rather than waiting passively for a feeling to motivate you. (from page 182)

We won't become so tired of doing what we do in life if we are more careful concerning how we think about our lives.

Scriptures to meditate on:

Matthew 11:28
1 Corinthians 2:16
2 Corinthians 10:4–5
Romans 8:1
Colossians 3:2

SECTION 4

How Your Thoughts Affect Your Walk with God

In the last section of *The Mind Connection*, we focus on our most important relationship—the one we have with God—and how our thoughts impact it. While we have been considering how God influences our thoughts throughout the book, in the last section we will focus more intentionally on our relationship with our God.

Take a few minutes to journal about where you currently stand with God. How is your relationship with Him? How deeply do you trust God? How often do you think about Him?

_____

_____

_____

_____

_____

Thinking About What God Thinks About You

Before you begin, familiarize yourself with chapter 18 of *The Mind Connection*.

Mind Check

How has your work on releasing energy-zapping habits and thoughts been going? What do you need to keep doing to have the energy you need to live well?

_____

_____

_____

What does it mean to have our confidence in Christ? How do you do it, practically speaking?

_____

_____

_____

_____

There are many voices that try to shape the way we think about every part of ourselves—our appearance, our abilities, our potential, and our identity. But those voices can be misleading. The opinions of the world, the accusations of our adversary, and our own thoughts and feelings don't define us.

The Bible teaches that the true identity, worth, and value of a believer is found in Christ. Our confidence is in Him (see Philippians 3:3). It doesn't matter what people think or say, or what our circumstances look like; we are defined by the fact that God loves and accepts us completely. To walk with God, we need to be in agreement with Him, and that involves learning to think as He thinks. (from page 191)

What are some other things you try to put your confidence in? (Such as money, your appearance, performance, reputation, etc.)

_____

_____

_____

The Mind Connection

Wrong thinking about ourselves can lead to what I refer to as a case of "mistaken identity."…When we have a case of mistaken identity, or we fail to know our worth and value as a child of God, we can also end up in prison. It may be an emotional prison of fear, self-hatred, poor self-image, lack of confidence, and many other unpleasant things. Jesus came to announce the release of the captives and the opening of the prison to those who are bound. (from pages 191–192)

Read the following Scriptures. In your own words, write what this says about you as a believer in Christ. How do these words shape your identity?

John 3:16

_____

_____

_____

Jeremiah 1:5

_____

_____

_____

Philippians 4:13

_____

_____

_____

Spend some time now thinking about how your identity in Christ can set you free from a negative self-image or thoughts about yourself.

_____

_____

_____

_____

_____

Make the Connection

Have you ever taken any time to consider what you think about yourself? Most people have not, but it is an important thing to do. I can remember desperately struggling for most of my life with myself, but I finally learned to see myself as God does, and it revolutionized my life. My father had told me I was no good and would never amount to anything, but God tells me that I am His and that through Him, I can do greater things than I could ever imagine. It really isn't what other people think about us that hurts us, but it is what we think of ourselves!

God by His grace changes us on the inside, and then the Holy Spirit works with us, teaching us to live inside out! We are made right with God through faith in Christ. We are sanctified, and that means we are set apart and made holy by Him. These and many other wonderful works are accomplished in our spirits by God's grace. It is His gift to us! When we learn to believe what God has done in us, we will produce the fruit of it in our daily lives.

We may not do everything right, but God views us as right through our faith in Jesus and His work on the cross for us. The world places labels and assigns varying values to almost everything, but to God we are all equal. He loves and values each of us equally. We are all one in Christ! (from pages 193–194)

Memorize some of the following Scriptures that remind you of what God thinks of you. Write affirmations based on them, and repeat them frequently so you can begin to think like God thinks about you! Consider writing your Scripture affirmations on note cards or on your phone or computer. Place them where you can see them often and be reminded of who you are in Christ.

Psalm 40:5

_____

_____

_____

Psalm 139:17–18

_____

_____

_____

Jeremiah 29:11

_____

_____

_____

The Word of God is what defines you, not the opinions of the world, the accusations of your adversary, or your own thoughts and feelings.

Scriptures to meditate on:

Genesis 1:31
Isaiah 55:8–9
Romans 8:37–39
Psalm 40:5

Thoughts and Behavior

Before you begin, familiarize yourself with chapter 19 of *The Mind Connection*.

Mind Check

How has remembering how God thinks of you helped change your thoughts about yourself? What results do you see in your actions?

_____

_____

_____

_____

_____

Think about the opening quote:

> Thoughts are boomerangs returning to their source. Choose wisely which ones you throw.

Which thoughts have you been throwing around in your head lately? How have they come back to you through your actions?

_____

_____

_____

God's Word says that we are to live as Christ lived, love as He loved, think with His mind, and feel what He feels. It sounds like a daunting task, and we often turn the task into a nightmare of frustration and failed effort simply because we try to be good while at the same time we have bad thoughts.

Behold my affliction and my pain and forgive all my sins [of thinking and doing]. Psalm 25:18

This Scripture makes it clear that sinful thinking precedes sinful behavior. We cannot change our behavior unless we are willing to first be accountable for the thoughts that we meditate on. (from page 202)

The Mind Connection

A walk consists of many steps. As we walk with God, these steps are decisions that we make along the way about many things. We should use our free will to choose God's will. When we make right choices, God's grace is always available to help us follow through. (from page 202)

How do you renew your mind? Try each of the ways listed below. Write what you will think about.

Declaring God's Word is one of the most effective ways to renew your mind. What do you need help with specifically this week? What Scriptures can remind you of what God says in this area?

The renewal of the mind also requires us to be willing to think about what we think about and to take wrong thoughts captive to the obedience of Christ. How can you stop wrong or negative thinking and take your thoughts captive?

_____

_____

_____

Read the Scriptures I suggest on pages 204–209. Which ones speak to you strongly or really grab your attention? List them below.

_____

_____

_____

There are multitudes of people who believe in Jesus, but they never experience victory in their lives due to a lack of knowledge or an unwillingness to apply the principles they have learned. I spent many years as a Christian who attended church regularly before ever discovering that my mind had anything to do with my behavior. I lacked knowledge. Then after acquiring the knowledge, I still had to be willing to go through the process, and I am still going through it even to this day. We will never have a day in our lives when we don't have to choose to cast down wrong thoughts and replace them with good ones.

The good news is that although it is quite a battle in the beginning, it does get easier as time goes by. We learn to recognize wrong and destructive thinking much quicker, and because we have learned the value of thinking properly, we can immediately choose thoughts that benefit us and help us enjoy God's plan for our lives. (from page 203)

Make the Connection

The Word of God has power in it to save our souls when we approach it with meekness (see James 1:21). You cannot change yourself, or force yourself to behave better, but you can ask God to help you, and

He will use His Word to grant you the strength and discipline that you need. God changes us from one degree of glory to another as we study His Word (see 2 Corinthians 3:18). We have already seen that with God's help we can choose to walk as Jesus walked (behave as He did). God's Word transforms us into the image of Jesus, and our behavior changes for the better. (from page 209)

What new affirmations can you make, based on Scripture, that will renew your mind in the areas in which you need to make improvements?

_____

_____

_____

_____

_____

The more you meditate on the Word of God, the more your mind is renewed.

Scriptures to meditate on:

Romans 12:2

Romans 8:5–6

Romans 13:14

James 1:21

2 Corinthians 3:18

The Mind-Mouth Connection

Before you begin, familiarize yourself with chapter 20 of *The Mind Connection*.

Mind Check

How has meditating on God's Word and speaking your affirmations from chapter 19 helped you?

_____

_____

_____

Which one has been on your mind the most? Explain why.

_____

_____

_____

On a scale of 1 to 10 (with 1 being never and 10 being all the time), rate how often your words are positive, uplifting, and considered encouraging to others. Explain your rating.

_____

_____

_____

The connection between what we think and what we say is stronger than most people realize. We will never change what we say if we don't understand how important what we say is!...Words are containers filled with power, and we choose whether that power will be negative or positive. We can bless or curse with the words of our mouth. We can build up or tear down. We can make people laugh or make them cry. God wants to use us to advance His Kingdom. He wants us to partner with Him in introducing people to Him, and just as we can learn to think as God does, we can also learn to talk as He talks. (page 213)

The Mind Connection

Read James 3. Describe what James says about the tongue.

_____

_____

_____

It was many years before I had any idea that my own thoughts and words had tremendous influence on my life and behavior. For example, due to being abused and controlled by my father, I repeatedly said to myself, as well as to others, "When I get out of this house, nobody is ever going to tell me what to do again." I became very rebellious toward authority, and especially male authority. When Dave and I got married, I learned in God's Word that God wanted me to respect and admire Dave's opinions and to honor him as the head of our home, but I was totally unable to do so. I wanted to, but I could not!

It took some time and some strong lessons from the Holy Spirit before I learned that I had imprisoned myself in rebellion by the words I said for years when I was younger. I had actually made a vow to myself that I would not let anyone ever tell me what to do. I finally saw my error and repented, asking God to forgive me and to soften my hardened heart toward authority. It took some time, but as I grew in God and changed my thinking and speaking, my mind was renewed and I was set free. (from pages 214–215)

What are some things you may have said when you were young that could perhaps be preventing you from breaking bad habits, like my addiction to cigarettes or disregard for authority?

_____

_____

_____

Write a prayer asking God to help change your thinking and to give you specific Scriptures in His Word that will renew your mind with positive thinking and enable you to take God-honoring actions.

_____

_____

_____

Words definitely have power. Many people with addictions say over and over that the addiction is too strong for them to break it or that they will never be free from it, and sure enough they end up being right. It would be most helpful for anyone trying to overcome an addiction or break any bad habit to begin confessing what they want to see happen, instead of confessing that they will never be free. (from page 215)

Make the Connection

Read the following Scriptures and write what they mean to you and how you can use them to have more control over your thoughts and words.

Romans 4:17

_____

_____

_____

Ephesians 5:1

_____

_____

_____

When we speak, our thought life is being turned inside out. If we don't want our thoughts to be revealed, then we better not think them too long, because if we do, they usually find a way to get out. Jesus said that what is in the heart comes out of the mouth (see Matthew 12:34), and Jesus is always right. It is not safe to keep thinking something if you really don't want to end up saying it. Of course, there is a chance you might control yourself and never say what you think, but I believe it is better not to take the chance. I think the connection between the mind and the mouth may be the strongest one we experience. When the two join together and are in agreement, the rest of our fate is sealed. If I think angry thoughts and speak angry words, I will begin to feel angry in my emotions, and more than likely I will display angry behavior toward someone before too long. The mind connection is powerful indeed! (from pages 217–218)

When you find your thinking drifting into an area that is negative, what can you say to get your focus back on God, His Word, and His heart for you? (For example, I say "I trust You, God" when I begin to worry.)

_____

_____

_____

What you allow yourself to meditate on and to declare influences your destiny.

Scriptures to meditate on:

Proverbs 18:21
Matthew 6:31
Matthew 12:34
1 Peter 3:10
Proverbs 22:17–18

How to Get Your Mind Back When You Feel Like You Have Lost It!

Before you begin, familiarize yourself with chapter 21 of *The Mind Connection*.

Mind Check

What have you been meditating on most? How has it affected what you say and how you feel?

_____

_____

_____

_____

How calm are you during a difficult time? Rate yourself from 1 to 10 (with 1 being not calm at all and 10 being totally calm). Explain your rating.

_____

_____

_____

In the midst of the storm, it's important to take inventory of your thoughts and release any that are stealing your peace. The next time you are in the middle of a storm, take an inventory of your thoughts.

I think we all have a tipping point and we can learn to recognize what it feels like when we are reaching it. You may be able to do two or even three things at one time, balancing them in such a way that they all get done without causing you stress, but at what point are you overwhelmed? What if the two or three things become ten things? Is that too much, or can you still take more?

We are each created differently, perfectly adapted for the call on our lives. I had an amazing ability to multitask in my earlier years because of what God had called me to do. The ministry was in the early, foundation-laying years, and the workload involved was quite heavy. Back in those days, let's say theoretically that I could easily handle juggling four problems at a time and still stay calm. Today that is different. I am older and in a different season of my life. Two is about my maximum these days. If I go over that, I start to feel that I am reaching my tipping point.

I have trained myself to recognize when I am on the verge of losing my peace, and I pull back and eliminate one of the things causing the problem. After almost forty years of experience walking with God, I know how important it is for me to keep my peace! By the way, God's Word doesn't say, "When you're upset, go get some peace," but it does say to "hold your peace" (see Exodus 14:14). (from pages 224–225)

The Mind Connection

Peace I leave with you; My [own] peace I now give and bequeath to you. Not as the world gives do I give to you. Do not let your hearts be troubled, neither let them be afraid. [Stop allowing yourselves to be agitated and disturbed; and do not permit yourselves to be fearful and intimidated and cowardly and unsettled.] John 14:27

This Scripture clearly places the responsibility for receiving His peace on us. Jesus has already given us peace. You may say, "Well, if that is true, then where is it, and why don't I feel peaceful?" You cannot wait to feel it in order to believe you have it. We access all the promises of God by believing them. God calls us to walk by faith and not by sight or feelings (see 2 Corinthians 5:7). I frequently say that we are like people trying to get into a chair we are already sitting in. Just imagine the uselessness and frustration of such an effort. If you're in the chair, then just relax and enjoy it. Jesus left us His peace, and if you believe it, you will begin to enjoy it. (from page 223)

What have you been consistently and constantly seeking God for? Do you have peace about the things you can't control or you're uncertain about?

_____

_____

_____

Look for Scriptures that speak directly to your requests and write them below.

_____

_____

_____

Are you asking for things God has already promised you and provided for you? How can you use your faith to access the things He has given but you haven't yet received? Write some practical, specific ways you can do this.

_____

_____

_____

_____

Make the Connection

Review the six steps I suggest you take when you feel you have lost your mind. Then rewrite them in your own words below and think of ways to help yourself remember each step.

If we don't make the decision to calm down early enough, then we will lose control, but even then it is not too late to regain control that has been lost. At any time we realize we are out of control, we can regain control by making a decision to do so. Here are some steps that will hopefully help in the process:

Step 1—Stop talking! When we feel overwhelmed, we usually start talking to anyone who will listen, and if nobody is around, we are prone to talking anyway just to hear the sound of our frustrations. We will never regain control unless we stop talking and regroup!

Step 2—Be as realistic as you can about what is really happening. Have you let yourself become more upset than the situation really calls for? Is the problem you are facing really as bad as you are imagining it to be? Are you worrying about things that have not even happened yet and may never happen?

Step 3—As you begin to calm down, ask yourself if any of the things you feel overloaded with can be put off until later or perhaps handed off to someone else to deal with. Could you get help if you ask for it? Are you really the only one who can handle the things pressuring you? Only a foolish person thinks they can keep doing the same thing and get a different result. So if you truly want change in your circumstances, you will have to be willing to make some changes yourself.

Step 4—Think about what you are thinking about that is frustrating you and stop thinking about it. Cast your care on God and let Him show you what He can do. Keep saying, "God, I let this go. I trust You!" Say it until you feel yourself calming down.

Step 5—We can manage our emotions and learn to live beyond our feelings. Being the master or mistress of yourself under God's leadership is entirely possible, but it will not happen as long as you let raw emotion rule. We cannot prevent feelings from coming, but we don't have to let them control us. We are totally capable of using self-control even in the midst of the wildest emotion. It may be painful to our soul, but it will be worth it in the end. Absolutely nobody respects him- or herself when they are out of control!

Step 6—Resist the devil at his onset! The root source of all lack of peace is the devil. It is not people or even circumstances. It is the devil working through the people or the circumstance. The devil has set you up to get you upset, and the sooner you realize it and take action to resist him, the easier it will be. (from pages 226–227)

_____

_____

_____

_____

_____

_____

_____

Jesus has already provided His peace. All you have to do is receive it.

Scriptures to meditate on:

2 Corinthians 5:7

Exodus 14:14

Deuteronomy 30:19

2 Timothy 1:7

Use the following note pages to remind yourself of what God has revealed to you while reading *The Mind Connection* and completing this study guide. Revisit these pages often to refresh and renew your mind. We truly know that the mind is connected to our outlook on life, our relationship with ourselves and others, and our relationship with our Lord and Savior, Jesus Christ. Renew your mind. Renew your thinking. Renew your life.

_____

_____

_____

_____

_____

_____

_____

_____

_____

_____

_____

_____

_____

_____

_____

_____

_____

_____

_____

Note Pages

JOYCE MEYER is one of the world's leading practical Bible teachers. Her TV and radio broadcast, *Enjoying Everyday Life*, airs on hundreds of television networks and radio stations worldwide.

Joyce has written more than 100 inspirational books. Her bestsellers include *Power Thoughts*; *The Confident Woman*; *Look Great, Feel Great*; *Starting Your Day Right*; *Ending Your Day Right*; *Approval Addiction*; *How to Hear from God*; *Beauty for Ashes*; and *Battlefield of the Mind*.

Joyce travels extensively, holding conferences throughout the year and speaking to thousands around the world.

Joyce Meyer Ministries—United States
P.O. Box 655
Fenton, MO 63026
USA
(636) 349-0303

Joyce Meyer Ministries—Canada
P.O. Box 7700
Vancouver, BC V6B 4E2
Canada
(800) 868-1002

Joyce Meyer Ministries—Australia
Locked Bag 77
Mansfield Delivery Centre
Queensland 4122
Australia
(07) 3349 1200

Joyce Meyer Ministries—England
P.O. Box 1549
Windsor SL4 1GT
United Kingdom
(0) 1753 831102

Joyce Meyer Ministries—South Africa
P.O. Box 5
Cape Town 8000
South Africa
(27) 21-701-1056